HAVANA
THE CITY AT A GLANCE

CW00793336

Teatro Nacional
Nicolás Arroyo and Gabriela Menér
building was finished in 1960 but o
in 1979. Visit for the art-strewn lobby, and the
top-floor bar's late-night gigs and iconic views.
Avenida Paseo y 39, T 879 6011

Ministerio de Relaciones Exteriores
The 1959 blue-glazed Foreign Ministry, by José
Fontan and Carlos Ferrer, stares out to sea
over the clam-shell roof of Estadio José Martí.
Calle Calzada 360 esq G

Edificio López Serrano
Ricardo Mira and Miguel Rosich designed the
vertical shafts and ziggurats of this 1932 art
deco hulk. Don't miss Enrique García Cabrera's
nickel-silver *El Tiempo* relief in the vestibule.
Calle 13, 106 entre L y M

Edificio FOCSA
This mighty winged beast was once one of the
world's largest reinforced concrete buildings.
Yet from afar, it appears ready for take-off.
See p010

Tryp Habana Libre
Castro and Guevara moved into the then-new
hotel after Cuba fell. History absolved them.
See p067

Ministerio de Comunicaciones
Long after Che's face first graced this square
(see p012), Camilo Cienfuegos showed up on
the old postal HQ. The question on everyone's
lips – how long before Fidel joins them?
Avenida Independencia esq Aranguren

Hospital Hermanos Ameijeiras
A bank turned into a hospital post-revolution,
it still houses the national vault in its bowels.
See p014

INTRODUCTION
THE CHANGING FACE OF THE URBAN SCENE

Cuba today is like one of its blushing *quinceañeras*, a teenager on the cusp of freedom from an overbearing father. How will she mature? Since Raúl Castro and then Miguel Díaz-Canel's succession, progress is afoot. To counter state job cuts in 2010, more than half a million self-employment licences have been issued, and the legalisation of ventures that attract the hallowed tourist dollar has created a small but previously unheard-of middle class (of 200 sanctioned professions, palm-tree pruner and 'dandy' have had less financial impact). Foreign investment is being courted, through golf resorts, a legion of joint-venture hotels and, more poignantly, a mega-port and special economic zone in Mariel, west of the capital, from where so many Cubans once floated away. Now they return from Miami by air, with much-needed hardware, iPhones and pockets full of cash.

As the country opens up, the fear is that the greenbacks and blue eyes will corrupt. On its 500th anniversary, Havana is unique in that much of its architecture is intact – each district is a showcase of the *en vogue* styles of its era – if photogenically decrepit. The colonial core is being restored (see p019) but the whole city is in dire need of protection. As it falls down around them, its inhabitants muddle on, and despite the hardship there's little crime, and a social sensibility embodied in Raúl's daughter, a LGBT champion. Change happens sluggishly here and is often a chimera. Habaneros shrug, and reason that while they wait, they may as well face the music and dance.

ESSENTIAL INFO
FACTS, FIGURES AND USEFUL ADDRESSES

TOURIST OFFICE
Infotur
Obispo 524 entre Bernaza y Villegas
T 801 4333
www.infotur.cu

TRANSPORT
Car hire
Rex
Línea esq Malecón
T 836 7788
www.rex.cu
Transtur
www.transturcarrental.com
Taxis
Cubataxi
T 855 5555
Almost every car on the street is a potential taxi; official ones have blue number plates. If there is no meter, agree a price first

EMERGENCY SERVICES
Ambulance
T 104
Fire
T 105
Police
T 106
24-hour pharmacy
Farmacia Internacional Miramar
Avenida 41, 1814 esq 20
T 204 4350

EMBASSIES
British Embassy
Calle 34, 702-704 esq 7ma
T 214 2200
www.ukincuba.fco.gov.uk
US Embassy
Calzada entre L y M
T 839 4100
cu.usembassy.gov

POSTAL SERVICES
Post office
Oficios 102 entre Lamparilla y Amargura
Shipping
DHL
Avenida 1ra y 26
T 204 1876

BOOKS
The Book of Havana edited by Orsola Casagrande (Comma Press)
Great Houses of Havana by Hermes Mallea (Monacelli Press)
Revolution of Forms: Cuba's Forgotten Art Schools by John A Loomis (Princeton Architectural Press)

WEBSITES
Architecture
www.arquitecturacuba.com
Art
www.bellasartes.co.cu
Newspaper
www.havanatimes.org

EVENTS
La Bienal de La Habana
www.bienalhabana.fcbc.cu
Festival of New Latin American Cinema
www.habanafilmfestival.com

COST OF LIVING
Taxi from José Martí Airport to Vedado
CUC25
Cappuccino
CUC2.5
Packet of cigarettes
CUC1.50
Daily newspaper
CUP0.20
Bottle of champagne
CUC60

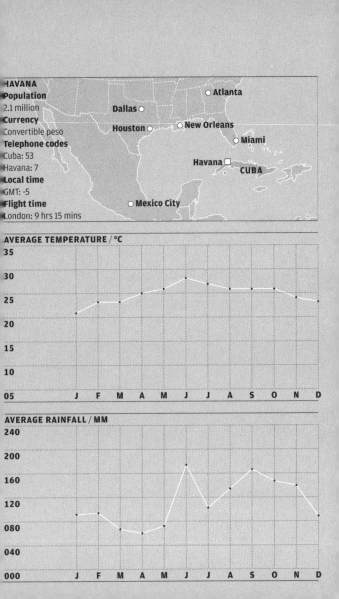

HAVANA

Population
2.1 million

Currency
Convertible peso

Telephone codes
Cuba: 53
Havana: 7

Local time
GMT: -5

Flight time
London: 9 hrs 15 mins

Atlanta
Dallas
Houston — New Orleans
Miami
Havana
CUBA
Mexico City

AVERAGE TEMPERATURE / °C

	J	F	M	A	M	J	J	A	S	O	N	D
35												
30												
25												
20												
15												
10												
05												

AVERAGE RAINFALL / MM

	J	F	M	A	M	J	J	A	S	O	N	D
240												
200												
160												
120												
080												
040												
000												

NEIGHBOURHOODS
THE AREAS YOU NEED TO KNOW AND WHY

To help you navigate the city, we've chosen the most interesting districts (see below and the map inside the back cover) and colour-coded our featured venues, according to their location; those venues that are outside these areas are not coloured.

PLAZA DE LA REVOLUCIÓN
This monumental expanse, built to impress in the 1950s by dictator Fulgencio Batista, was commandeered by Castro for the same purpose. It's loosely enclosed by ministries, cultural venues and an obelisk memorial to José Martí (see p015), who is as much a revolutionary hero as the two 'C's. Among all this puffed-out-chest architecture are sweet touches of everyday life, such as the musicians practising among the trees.

MIRAMAR
The first bridge across the Río Almendares was finished in 1910, and by the 1940s the rich were moving west to build mansions along the wide avenues. It is still well-off. Restaurants like La Fontana (Calle 3ra A esq 46, T 202 8337) attract diplomats, foreign businessmen and the in-crowd. Also check out the delightful La Esperanza (Calle 16, 105 entre 1ra y 3ra, T 202 4361) and hip nightspots such as Espacios (see p045).

HABANA VIEJA
In 1519, the city was founded here, and the unique melange of colonial architecture became a World Heritage Site in 1982. It's a mix of baroque, Moorish and art nouveau flourish that is half ruined, half restored. In the early evening, main drag Obispo is a riot of salsa, live music, shops and hustlers ('Oye, amigo, where you fron?'), and Plaza Vieja has been returned to its former glory. Yet, off the beaten path, crumbling facades are kept up by makeshift wooden beams.

LA RAMPA
Rising from the Malecón up to ice-cream palace Coppelia (see p031), La Rampa was the hub of 1950s cavorting and is still a strut for locals of all persuasions. It bustles with offices, shops, cafés, cinemas and matinee venues, and La Zorra y El Cuervo (La Rampa entre N y O, T 833 2402) is an intimate jazz haunt. Many decent paladares line Calle M, and club Salon Rojo (Calle 21 entre N y O, T 833 3747) hosts reggaeton and salsa acts.

VEDADO
After the sugar price spiked due to WWI, the bourgeoisie built their villas here in Italianate and neoclassical styles, with gardens, fountains and sculptures – the Museo de Artes Decorativas (see p033) is a superb example. Later decades saw the arrival of the art deco Casa de las Américas (see p082) and the 1950s Hotel Riviera (see p074). It is a cultured, tranquil part of the city, with theatres, museums and parks.

CENTRO
Havana's heart is a dense jumble of lost elegance and lives played out in public, and by night its unlit streets are other-worldly. The 1927 Compañia Cubana de Teléfonos (Aguila 565) is a terracotta-iced confection next to Chinatown, while Parque Central is bordered by hotels, the 1915 Gran Teatro (Paseo de Martí 458, T 861 3077), home to the ballet, and the Capitolio (see p009). Grand old El Prado, centre of the nascent housing market, shuffles down to the sea.

LANDMARKS
THE SHAPE OF THE CITY SKYLINE

The best way to get a handle on Havana is to brave the rickety lifts of the 123m Edificio FOCSA (overleaf) or the 113m Memorial José Martí (see p015). From these two lookouts you see a city virtually unaltered since 1959. The lack of modern skyscrapers does mean that the few high rises that do exist stand out on the flat skyline, which is useful, as asking locals for directions is generally fruitless. Dominating Parque Central is the 91m dome of the incongruous 1929 Capitolio Nacional (Industria y Barcelona). Built on US credit and regarded as an imperialist folly, after a long renovation begun in 2012, it now surprisingly houses the Cuban National Assembly. Elsewhere, the Habana Libre (see p067) rises above La Rampa; the striped Meliá Cohiba (see p016) signals the Vedado seafront; and the Embajada de Rusia (see p011) is the unloved beacon of Miramar.

Another useful anchor is the hub of Plaza de la Revolución, a mammoth town-planning initiative of the early 1950s, from which boulevards fan out to all corners. This was only the first stage of urban development – Castro's arrival in Havana actually preserved the city, as it nixed a 1956 proposal by famed Catalan architect Josép Lluís Sert, and other ideas yet more radical, that advocated razing the axes of Habana Vieja to replace them with tower blocks. In fact, so little has changed in six decades that today Havana is as much about its crumbling architecture as those who have to live with it. *For full addresses, see Resources.*

Edificio FOCSA

The 33 floors of Cuba's tallest residential structure topped out in 1956. It was devised in a bird-in-flight shape by Ernesto Gómez Sampera and Martín Domínguez, and the Le Corbusian plans included a cinema, TV studios, offices and a pool. There was little consideration of the urban context in those heady times, as is seen in the foreground, where two eclectic-style mansions, one of which houses El Gato Tuerto (T 838 2696), an intimate bolero haunt, are dwarfed by the green concrete giant. Post-revolution, many of FOCSA's privileged residents fled; its pool has lain empty for decades and has hosted many an impromptu baseball game. However, top-floor restaurant/bar La Torre (T 838 3089) remains one of the city's most upmarket old-school venues, so long as the elevator happens to be working. *Calle 17 entre M y N*

Embajada de Rusia

The 20-storey tower of the 1985 Russian Embassy is a striking, if sinister, triumph of ideologically charged architecture by Alexander Rochegov. The concrete-and-glass complex thrusts above the mansions of Miramar, converted into consulates and government offices post-revolution. As if a one-fingered salute to the USA across the water, the embassy's unique melodrama evokes the space race. It was once home to hundreds of Soviet comrades, but now little is left of their legacy, save the stretch Ladas bouncing over the city's potholes. These days a skeleton staff rattles around inside, with time to skid across the marble and contemplate Lenin set in stained glass, as well as murals by Rochegov's daughter, Anna. As with so much of Havana, it is a poignant reminder of Cuba's lost history.
Avenida 5ta, 6402 entre 62 y 66

Ministerio del Interior
This 1953 building by Aquiles Capablanca,
clad in Jaimanitas stone and brise-soleil,
and with a ceramic mural by Amelia Peláez,
is the most successful in the Plaza de la
Revolución. But the Ministry of the Interior
only achieved tourist-trap status with the
1993 addition of a 30m frieze of old boss
Che to the concave elevator block. Based
on the 1960 Alberto Korda photo, flesh was
made steel behind the spot where Castro
gave a speech after Guevara was killed in
1967. It carries the slogan *Hasta la Victoria
Siempre* and lights up at night. In 2009,
Guevara was joined by fellow hero Camilo,
who adorns Ernesto Gómez Sampera's
1954 Ministerio de Comunicaciones.
Despite also being designed by sculptor
Enrique Ávila, the craftsmanship is less
accomplished and he appears rather
cartoon-like – perhaps symbolic of the
current state of the revolutionary ideals.
Avenida Céspedes esq Aranguren

Hospital Hermanos Ameijeiras

The largest hospital in Cuba sticks out like a sore thumb in low-rise Centro. The 23-storey flanked tower of yellowy Jaimanitas stone and the expansive plaza overlooking the Malecón suggest big bucks, and indeed construction began under Batista when it was intended to be the National Bank, with the lobby housing a stock exchange. Post-revolution, it was decided that the unfinished building should provide a more worthy purpose. Original architect Nicolás Quintana was forced to leave the country in 1960 after falling out with bank president Guevara over plans that he considered to be impractical for a hospital, and latterly called it a 'crude hybrid'. It was eventually inaugurated in 1982 with the best facilities on the island, yet the archaic US embargo has resulted in a chronic lack of medicine.
San Lázaro y Belascoaín

Memorial José Marti

This tribute to Cuba's spiritual godfather is the centrepiece of Plaza de la Revolución's monumental symbolism. The star-shaped grey marble spire is deceptively tall (141m with spike) and you can see for 60km from the top – not *quite* as far as the relatives in Miami. Architect Aquiles Maza and sculptor Juan José Sicre won the competition for its design, but after Batista came to power he commissioned third-placed Enrique Luis Varela, his political crony. An outcry led to the addition of Sicre's 18m statue at its base. Construction began in 1953, the centenary of Marti's birth, and took five years. Behind it is the Communist Party HQ, in the 1957 Palacio de Justicia, ironically an Italian fascist-style design by José Pérez Benitoa & Sons. The vast plaza itself is used for political rallies and papal visits.

Avenida Paseo y Independencia

HOTELS

WHERE TO STAY AND WHICH ROOMS TO BOOK

Since reforms in 1993, Cuba has embraced tourism as its cash cow, leading to the rebirth of a raft of colonial properties as boutique hotels (see p019), often with a kitsch theme. As the city approached its 500th anniversary in 2019, the state majorly upped the ante with high-profile behemoths run as joint ventures with European chains opening on Prado, such as the Kempinski (see p060) and Iberostar Grand Packard (51 Paseo de Martí, T 823 2100), and big builds along the Malecón (see p087), and facing the tired Tryp Habana Libre (see p067). Like the older heavyweights – the Meliá Cohiba (Avenida Paseo entre 1ra y 3ra, T 833 3636) and Parque Central (Neptuno esq Zulueta, T 860 6627) – they have wi-fi and all the facilities, but their sterility robs you of the Cuban experience, be that good or bad, and considering the parlous state of the economy, prices are high. As for the Miramar resorts, leave them in their seafront car parks.

Far more enticing is a clutch of bijou privately owned, expertly converted micro-'hotels' with just a handful of rooms, in which the service is second to none, exemplified by Economía 156 (see p022) and Loma de Ángel (see p018), which was the first to launch in 2016. They're a natural extension of the *casa particular* phenomenon (see p023) – and renting a room in a Cuban home remains an authentic and hugely rewarding experience, and a genuine help to locals. Or you could just get the keys to your own penthouse (see p087). *For full addresses and room rates, see Resources.*

Hotel Saratoga

For interior design, calm and convenience, this might still be the best headline hotel in town. The eclectic neoclassical shell dates from the 1880s, and the place was a high-society haunt in the 1930s. It reopened in 2005 with two extra floors, reproduction features and a palm-bedecked atrium bar with a mural by Juan Carlos Botello, which hosts live music in the early evening, and is a chilled spot to get online, whether or not you're staying. Of the 96 rooms, the best are the huge Habana Suites, with swathes of Cuban marble and mahogany, claw-foot tubs and wraparound balconies. Service is close to European level, there is a gym and spa, and the rooftop pool (above), bar and restaurant was the city's first, revamped in 2019, and looks out to the Capitolio dome. *Prado 603 esq Dragones, T 868 1000, www.hotel-saratoga.com*

La Reserva Vedado

Three European architects converted this typically eclectic El Vedado mansion, from 1914, with its Corinthian columns, repetitive arches, high ceilings and ornate tiles, into a boutique hotel/*casa particular* hybrid. Interventions, notably a floating staircase and a metal and bamboo bar among the banana and avocado trees in the garden, complement the restored features, as do works by contemporary artists, including Juan Roberto Diago Durruthy and Damián Aquiles (see p054). Antique dressers and wardrobes lend the 11 rooms a homely feel: the best, like the Malecon, Coppelia and Presidente (above), have private terraces. In Miramar, Le Petit Mistinguett (T 5284 1489) is a similar venture with five rooms in a gorgeous 1957 midcentury residence. *Calle 2, 508 entre 21 y 23, T 833 5244, www.lareservavedado.com*

Hotel Florida

Arguably the most accomplished of the many Habana Vieja renovations, Florida is in the thick of the Calle Obsipo melee, but once you settle into a wicker chair in its two-tiered, porticoed atrium (above), peace will descend. The 1836 noble-family residence retains an elegant intimacy, and its 25 spacious colonial-style rooms have wrought-iron beds and furnishings, lofty beamed ceilings and chequerboard marble floors. Other highlights of the government's restoration programme, led by the brilliant city historian Eusebio Leal, are the massive stained-glass lobby roof in the art nouveau Hotel Raquel (T 860 8280); the 1784 Santa Isabel (T 860 8201) in Plaza de Armas; and Palacio del Marqués de San Felipe (T 801 1190), which has a contemporary interior.
Obispo 252 esq Cuba, T 862 4127,
www.gaviotahotels.com

Loma del Ángel

With its narrow streets, cute squares and well-tended brightly painted houses, Loma de Ángel is a surprisingly tranquil enclave in the usually cacaphonic old town. It's also the setting of the climactic scene in Cirilo Villaverde's 1839 novel *Cecilia Valdés*, an inspiration for this bijou hideaway. Behind its early 19th-century facade, three storeys have been totally remodelled. Interiors by Barcelona studio Federico Crocellà have a black and white scheme that extends from the tiled floor to the iron staircase, painted wood doors and trim of the Egyptian cotton sheets. Above the reception and breakfast area, detailed with reupholstered French chairs and vintage Asian items, are just two well-appointed, wonderfully stylish rooms, one on each floor (Terrace Suite, above). *Cuarteles 104, T 801 5585, www.lomadelangel.com*

Economía 156

The neglected south part of Habana Vieja is on its way up (in relative terms – the roads have now been paved) with the overhaul of the train station to serve the reborn Mariel docks. Here, film and theatre directors Jazz Martinez-Gamboa and Stephen Bayly found a collapsing 1906 townhouse and replaced the rotting roof and floors with concrete (also used to build a hi-spec kitchen) and restored the ceiling beams, ironwork and pretty tiles. The exquisite 2018 result, from the front salon to the three rooms (master, above) leading off a passageway, and a roof deck with bougainvillea climbing a pergola, is enhanced by a super concierge and guide service and a killer breakfast. On parallel street Cárdenas, known for its extravagant art nouveau, is hip gallery Arsenal (No 51).
Economía 156 entre Gloria y Misión,
T 861 3211, www.economia156.com

Villa María

Cuba's unique economic model deserves credit for the rise of the global sharing culture, from Airbnb to pop-up eateries. When *casas particulares* were legalised in 1997, locals rented out the granny room or bumped the kids. Now you can relax in a 1950s Vedado penthouse at Artedel (T 830 8727) and, since 2010, even get the keys to your own flat or mansion. Many properties have a fine architectural pedigree, prices compare to those at the top hotels and, if you want creature comforts, simply employ a chef. Villa María (aka Farah) is a covetable 1940 six-bedroom mansion by the mouth of the Río Almendares, with minimal interiors, a kidney-shaped pool and a built-in bar. The lovely sweep of the balustraded staircase deservedly has star billing. Rent the whole house (families only) or one of the rooms. *T 362 0667, www.havanacasaparticular.com*

24 HOURS

SEE THE BEST OF THE CITY IN JUST ONE DAY

Many a soul has spent an entire 24 hours here partying (famously, Hemingway) and abstinence is nigh-on impossible. It's equally easy to achieve nothing – Cubans have made an art form of it – yet you need to be organised, as the top restaurants require a booking and 'official' business invariably takes an eternity, even having an ice cream at Coppelia (see p031). In addition, the architectural sights such as those in fascinating Centro (see p079), and the Cementerio (see p078) and art schools (see p102), are strung out, although it's possible to reach most on an open-top tourist bus, could you bear the shame. If you hail a taxi, don't count on the driver having the faintest idea where he's going – he's probably a nuclear engineer.

Cultural life is one thing that's rich in Cuba. Happenings and gigs, often last-minute or off-the-cuff, take place in all manner of venues, including Salón Rosado de la Tropical (Avenida 41 y 46, T 203 5322), Sálon Rojo (Calle 21 entre N y O, T 833 3747), FAC (see p038) and Teatro Bertolt Brecht (see p080), so ask around to find *la cosa buena*. You'll be aware of the old-time musos but look out for the new breed: pianists Harold López-Nussa and Roberto Fonseca; singers Danay Suárez, Eme Alfonso and Diana Fuentes; Descemer Bueno (fusion); Ogguere (hip hop); Gente de Zona (reggaeton); and Cimafunk.

And remember that if you encounter any obstacles in Havana, even a modest *propina* (tip) will get you an extremely long way. *For full addresses, see Resources.*

10.00 Museo de la Revolución

You can't escape politics in Cuba, so get up to speed with the exhaustive displays inside the 1920 former Presidential Palace, a riot of classical allusions and Spanish revival overtones by Rodolfo Maruri and Belgian Paul Belau. The Salón de los Espejos (Hall of Mirrors; above) was used for lavish state receptions and has interiors by Tiffany & Co, as well as an enormous ceiling painting by Cuban Armando Menocal. Engaging exhibits include the tiny suit of astronaut Arnaldo Tamayo Méndez (the first Latino in space). Fidel Castro's ex-security chief claimed there were 638 attempts on his life, and some hapless, Bond-style CIA plots are revelled in, from exploding cigars to a poisoned wetsuit, as well as shoe polish meant to make Castro's distinctive beard fall out, destroying his power, à la Samson. *Refugio 1 esq Misiones, T 862 2463*

10.45 Museo Nacional de Bellas Artes

The country's best collection of Cuban art is housed in a modernist block designed by Alfonso Rodríguez Pichardo. It opened in 1954 and is an exemplar of the synthesis of art and architecture that Latin America does so well, with sculpture by Rita Longa at the entrance and balconies displaying pieces by Mateo Torriente, Teodoro Ramos Blanco and Ernesto González. The galleries are arranged chronologically across three floors around an internal patio. Look for modern classics including Victor Manuel García's *Gitana Tropical*, Carlos Enrique's *El Rapto de las Mulatas* and Wifredo Lam's *Maternidad*. Contemporary highlights are *Corazón Que No Siente* by Flavia Garciandía, *Paisaje Cubano* by Kcho and *Estadística* by Tania Bruguera. Closed Mondays. *Trocadero entre Monserrate y Zulueta, T 862 0140, www.bellasartes.co.cu*

12.00 Malecón

Considering Havana's regular buffeting by hurricanes, sea defences were crucial to the development of the city. US engineers Mead and Whitney began the Malecón in 1901 at Castillo de la Punta and progress inched along, reaching La Rampa in 1923 and eventually the Río Almendares in 1959 to link with the new Miramar tunnel. The porticoed buildings along the Centro part have been ravaged by erosion but a few are now being restored into stylish spaces like hotel Malecón 663 (T 860 1459) where you should stop for coffee. From here, it's a short walk to Callejón de Hamel (overleaf). Dusk signals a mass human migration to the promenade, and all aspects of Cuban life are played out over countless bottles of rum, on 'the longest sofa in the world'. As a social scene it is far from homogeneous, and each stretch has its own conventions.

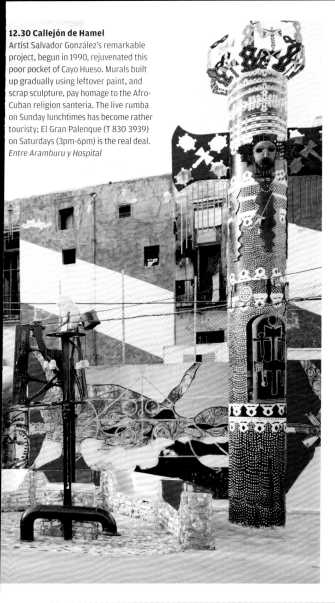

12.30 Callejón de Hamel

Artist Salvador González's remarkable project, begun in 1990, rejuvenated this poor pocket of Cayo Hueso. Murals built up gradually using leftover paint, and scrap sculpture, pay homage to the Afro-Cuban religion santeria. The live rumba on Sunday lunchtimes has become rather touristy; El Gran Palenque (T 830 3939) on Saturdays (3pm-6pm) is the real deal.
Entre Aramburu y Hospital

13.00 Café Laurent

This slick operation occupies the fifth-floor penthouse of a typical 1950s Vedado block, designed by Alberto Prieto. The layout has barely altered, from the curved corners to the home cocktail bar, which makes it even more fascinating – an old bedroom is now a private dining space and the bathroom is exactly that. There is a cream and brown palette, period furniture and a wall covered with pages from 1950s kitchen magazines.

Chef Ernesto Montells' well-executed fusion menu is typified by dishes such as seafood-stuffed peppers, and *sabor cubano* (roast pork with black bean cream). Dine on the lovely terrace, which has great views over the area and to the 1932 art deco Edificio López Serrano. A word of warning – get out of the lift on the wrong floor and you'll walk straight into someone's apartment.
Calle M 257 entre 19 y 21, T 831 2090

14.30 Coppelia

The ice cream sold here is one of few post-revolution luxuries, Castro's let-them-eat-cake gift to the people. Fidel himself was obsessed with it (Colombian writer Gabriel García Márquez once saw him eat 18 scoops at lunch). The futuristic concrete pavilion, a design by Mario Girona, was prefabricated and assembled in just six months, opening in 1966. The vaulted upper level (above) is sectioned off with wood and coloured glass and its spidery arms stretch out into a park shaded by banyan trees. There's space for 1,000 customers yet still there are queues for the day's flavours (there were originally 26, but now perhaps 10 if you're lucky); it's an unmissable slice of urban theatre. Note that foreigners are corralled towards a van where you pay in CUC, but if you have local pesos, join the long line. Closed Mondays. *Calle 23 y L*

15.30 Galería Villa Manuela

The gallery of the fabled Union of Writers and Artists of Cuba (UNEAC), a collective formed in 1961 that was instrumental in guiding Castro's cultural policy, opened to the public in 2004. It promotes the work of its hundreds of members, from art school graduates to leading contemporary figures including Rocío García, Marta María Pérez Bravo, René Peña and Florencio Gelabert. The standard is high (exhibition proposals must be submitted a year in advance) and some pieces are for sale. Weekdays, 10am to 5pm (it tends to close earlier). Next door, UNEAC itself occupies the 1920 home of a banker who topped himself on the eve of the revolution. Its garden often hosts live trova, rumba or jazz at 5pm on Wednesdays and bolero nights on Saturdays at 9pm. *Calle H 406 entre 17 y 19, T 832 2391, www.villamanuela.com*

16.30 Museo de Artes Decorativas

José Gómez Mena invented the mall in Cuba and, with the profits, commissioned a villa from French architects Viard et Dastugue and interiors by Jansen in Paris. Finished in 1927, the 11 rooms lead off the balconied double-height vestibule (above), with its switchback stairs, skylight, Carrara marble and bronze- and gold-plated decorative ironwork. Mena's sister, a countess, threw society do's here, showing off the Sèvres and the Wedgwood in the Regency dining room. The owners fled in 1961, stashing their worldly goods in the basement. The house was restored in 2003 and turned into a repository for decorative arts with some 35,000 pieces. Most interesting are the original rooms, notably the art deco bathroom with the tub built into an alcove. Closed Sundays and Monday afternoons. *Calle 17, 502 esq D, T 830 9848*

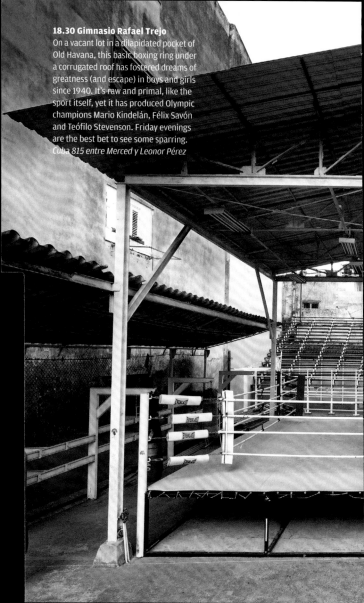

18.30 Gimnasio Rafael Trejo
On a vacant lot in a dilapidated pocket of
Old Havana, this basic boxing ring under
a corrugated roof has fostered dreams of
greatness (and escape) in boys and girls
since 1940. It's raw and primal, like the
sport itself, yet it has produced Olympic
champions Mario Kindelán, Félix Savón
and Teófilo Stevenson. Friday evenings
are the best bet to see some sparring.
Cuba 815 entre Merced y Leonor Pérez

19.45 Estadio Latinoamericano

Baseball was brought to Cuba in the 1860s by US dockers loading sugar in Matanzas. When the Spanish banned it in favour of bullfighting, the game became a symbol of defiance cemented in the national psyche. It remains incredibly popular – bring a bat and you could start an innings in an empty parking space (it's not difficult to find one). 'El Latino' opened in 1946 in working-class Cerro (before everywhere became working class) and is the largest ballpark in the Caribbean – 60,000 saw Cuba beat the States here in 1961. Home to Industriales (the Blue Lions, hence the paint job), its concrete mesh allows ventilation, and the laddered floodlights peer in at the action. Games usually start at 7.15pm during the August to January season. It's all raucously good fun, often aided by smuggled-in rum. *Pedro Pérez 302, T 873 2527*

21.15 Atelier

This was the first *paladar* since the classic La Guarida (see p049) to truly show what could be achieved. The late 18th-century mahogany-roofed villa, once owned by a senator, was acquired in a house swap and opened as Atelier in 2010, helped by its proximity to two huge hotels but never losing sight of the detail. Antique furniture and heirlooms pique the interest; large, well-spaced tables are laid with 1950s crockery and Murano glassware; and walls are hung with striking pieces by René Peña (above) and Moisés Finalé. The day's menu is printed on stock-take slips. The seafood soup is a frequent highlight and the rabbit and duck dishes are legendary. Wafted by the ocean breeze and a chilled soundtrack, the terrace exudes an Ibiza-esque vibe.
Calle 5ta, 511 altos entre Paseo y 2,
T 836 2025

23.00 Fábrica de Arte Cubano (FAC)

The phenomenon of FAC is evident from the hundreds clamouring to get in before it hits capacity. It's run by X Alfonso, who grew up in a famous musical dynasty surrounded by creatives and this is a natural extrapolation on a massive scale, a remarkable coming-together of popular culture, accessible to all (entry is CUC2). In a disused factory (see p056) leased from the state, fluidly divided and multi-layered, there are happenings everywhere: live gigs and DJs, screenings (including premieres), myriad exhibitions, dance and theatre performances, catwalk shows and design pop-ups. Since launch in 2014, it has often hosted headline events in Havana's many annual festivals, from jazz to cinema. Every three months it closes to refresh, prepare and launch the next cycle. Open Thursdays to Sundays, 6pm to 2am. *Calle 26 esq 11, T 838 2260, www.fac.cu*

URBAN LIFE
CAFÉS, RESTAURANTS, BARS AND NIGHTCLUBS

Cuban food has long had a bad reputation as low set wages ate away at any incentive to please customers. Yet that old joke: 'What are the three failures of the revolution? Breakfast, lunch and dinner' is no longer valid, as the grassroots *paladares* initially based in private homes have rewritten the recipe book, especially since bureaucracy was relaxed in 2011. Cuisine is market-driven in the extreme. Menus change daily because who knows what will be in the *agromercados*. At least the provenance is guaranteed, except for that of the hallowed beef and lobster, which arrive via the back door, and much of the produce will be organic, simply because chemicals are unaffordable. Given all the obstacles, the standard of many kitchens is superb.

Cutting-edge gigs and nightlife happen in off-the-radar dives and large venues on the city outskirts. Anywhere with a pool is also popular. A mythical info line lists the night's action – good luck with that as the number regularly changes (there are some listings at www.suenacubano.com). One thing that never will is Cabaret Tropicana (Calle 72, 4505, T 267 1717). It's a CUC100 sting, but Max Borges Recio's 1951 telescopic vaults are a triumph of function and location. You've come for the architecture, right? The latest fad is a happening cocktail scene on Havana's rooftops, at El Surtidor (see p060), El Cocinero (see p056), La Guarida (see p049), Malecón 663 (see p027), which hosts live jazz, and hip El del Frente (see p046). *For full addresses, see Resources.*

5 Sentidos

With a central open kitchen run by a team of chefs, the focus of this quality *paladar* is clear. It reinterprets traditional recipes through a global filter, seen in dishes such as *ropa vieja* arancini, marinated pork belly with passionfruit sauce, snapper ceviche, spiced smoked rabbit, and guava spheres filled with cream cheese mousse. Opened in 2017 in a 1920s neoclassical building on a prime corner site, its ingenious mezzanine level and Juan Carlos Polo's iron artworks on the walls are visible through the huge windows, and railing designs depict the five senses. It's popular, so book a few days in advance (a new phenomenon in Cuba). Also try the fusion cuisine at nearby Ivan Chefs Justo (T 863 9697) and the *léchon* at its sister *parrilla* Al Carbón downstairs. *San Juan de Dios 67 esq Compostela, T 864 8699, www.paladar5sentidos.com*

Río Mar

Not being commercially minded, Havana has few waterfront venues, so when this *paladar* opened in 2012 with a terrace by the river mouth it was on a promise. Río Mar backed it up with great seafood, frappé cocktails, a wine cellar and slick service. Rivalling the views are the glass chromatics, mosaic tiles and understated style of the 'private' room (pictured).
Avenida 3ra, 11 entre C y Final, T 209 4838

Café Madrigal

Filmmaker Rafael Rosales' intriguing home is crammed with the paraphernalia of three and a half decades spent in Cuban cinema. In 2011, he opened it up as a tapas bar (6pm to 2am, closed Mondays), its name derived from a backdrop to the Havana-set movie *Madrigal* that covers one wall (above). The cleverly lit bare bricks of the eclectic 1919 townhouse are decorated with film posters, antiques and Javier Guerra's revolutionary iconography. It is a natural home for the *farándula* – the bobo thespian in-crowd. In the park up the road, a John Lennon statue was unveiled in 2000 by Fidel in a 'Let It Be' gesture, 36 years after he banned The Beatles. Opposite is rock haunt the Yellow Submarine Club, and, as an odd Brit-mania takes hold, island-impounded locals have adopted the Union Jack as street fashion. *Calle 17, 809 altos entre 2 y 4, T 831 2433*

Espacios

This convivial haunt makes a big deal of its valet service, which, considering the wide, half-empty street outside and absence of crime in Cuba, is rather endearing. But in a way you can see why. This is tony Miramar, the only corner of this socialist country in which there are cars to actually park. It's a novelty – much like the late-night fast-food joint La Pachanga (T 830 2507), which got so rammed it built a VIP room. Espacios is far more than a glorified garage, of course. It is set in a mansion seemingly still lived in – arriving feels as if you're gatecrashing a fabulous house party. Multiple rooms are filled with art, antiques and quirky objects, and hefty helpings of tapas are served. But really it all happens after-hours in the back garden, where there's a cocktail bar, tinkly fountain and films projected on to the wall. *Calle 10, 513 entre 5ta y 7ma, T 202 2921*

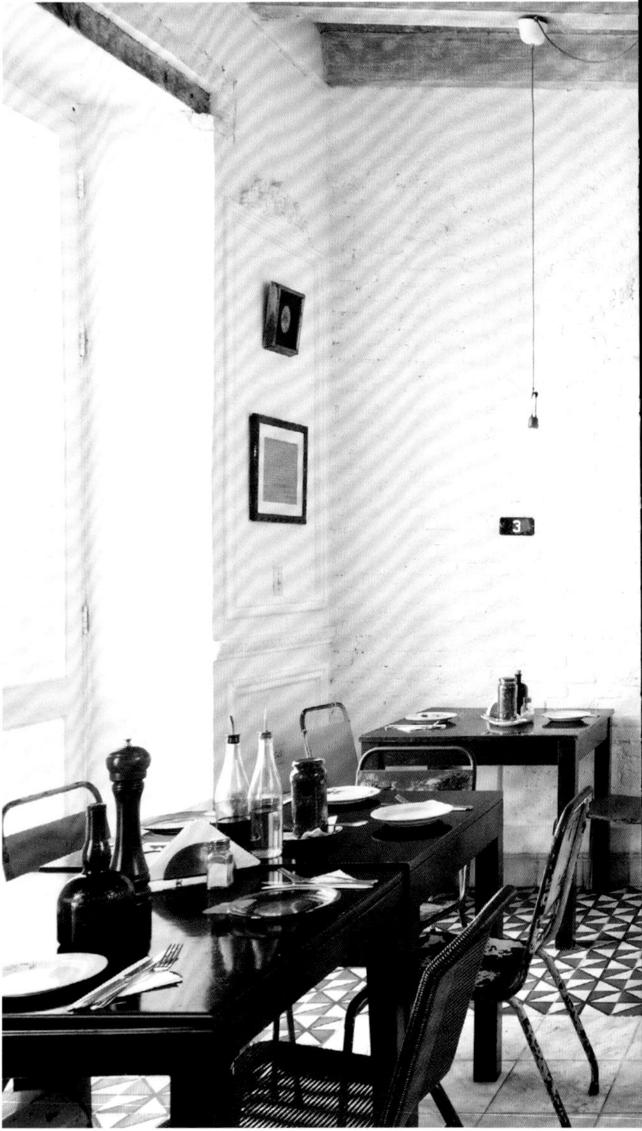
3

El del Frente

The 2016 follow-up to buzzy restaurant/bar O'Reilly 304 (T 863 0206), directly opposite (hence the name), has equally creative cocktails mixed in potato jars and new-world and Med cuisine such as ceviche, tuna tataki, seafood pasta and tacos served on vintage plates; and the hot sauce is a signature too. Add in a Brit obsession and the vibiest terrace in town.
O'Reilly 303 esq Aguiar, T 5237 7533

Casa de la Música Galiano

Since 1941, the lexicon of Cuban music has graced this showbiz palace. The immense art deco América Building was designed as a residential and entertainment complex (inspired by Radio City in New York) by Fernando Martínez Campos and Pascual de Rojas. The variety theatre's zodiac-motif lobby flooring, split double staircase and leather-upholstered anterooms are period pieces, but the dancefloor action is next door in Casa de la Música (above), which puts on live salsa and timba from the likes of Los Van Van; regular matinees featuring cubaton are mobbed by locals. Classic label Egrem also runs the touristy sister venue in Miramar (T 204 0447) and hosts intimate acoustic gigs at El Jelengue de Areito (T 862 0673; 5pm-9pm), on the patio outside the studios in which Buena Vista recorded.
Galiano 267 esq Neptuno, T 862 4165

Casa Miglis

Gregarious Swede Michel Miglis has worked in Cuban film and pop for decades, and with Andreas Hegert he has devised an inspired mash-up here. The restaurant has a loose Gustavian style that melds with the original 1922 tiles and high ceiling. National design classics such as the Ericofon are framed on walls (even IKEA gets a look-in) and used as tableware, and the menu features toast Skagen, meatballs, and lamb with yogurt and red wine. The bar has a 1950s carved counter, and salvaged chairs mounted on pipes that attest to local ingenuity. There's a dinner show by dancers Havana Queens in high season and an upstairs lounge opens until 2am every night. Centro's other major draws, La Guarida (T 866 9047) and Michifú (T 862 4869), are only a few blocks away. *Lealtad 120 entre Ánimas y Laguna, T 864 1486, www.casamiglis.com*

Hecho en Casa

Meaning 'homemade', charming Hecho en Casa is Alina Menéndez's mission to salvage the reputation of Cuban cuisine for being bland and fried by reviving classic flavours and celebrating its 'Creole melting pot' of influences. Inspired by the cooking of her Spanish grandmother, she started out in 2011 with a sandwich and juice stall, and added deserts such as *natilla de la abuela*, which is made by her mother and often on the chalkboard menu here (note prices are in Cuban pesos), as are *vegetales a la crema*, corn tamale with black-bean purée, prawn casserole remoulade and artisan ice cream. The experience is educational and informal, from the arrival drinks on the patio to the seven tables over two floors and a terrace, regularly attended to by Menéndez herself. *Calle 14, 511 entre 5ta y 7ma, T 202 5393, www.hechoencasa.com*

Restaurante 1830

This supperclub complex, in a neoclassical mansion on a promontory at the mouth of the Almendares, is named after the year it was born. Interiors are part restored, part eclectic; original iron grilles, turn-of-last-century chairs, chandeliers and fireplaces, and art deco-style stained glasswork in the library, now Bar Colonial, which is a refined spot for a sharpener. A red carpet leads in to an array of dining rooms, with a Cuban/ French menu and dishes such as prawns flambéed in rum. Despite a major revamp in 2019, the state-run establishment is often half-deserted. However, hidden behind it is Los Jardines, which has a Japanese-themed island that's plastered in shells (don't ask), and attracts some excellent dancers to its Sunday evening live salsa sessions under the stars. Call ahead to check the schedule.
Malecón 1252 y 22, T 838 3090

Otramanera

Secluded behind an imposing Corten-steel gate, this supremely accomplished *paladar* is a tranquil escape from the city hustle, set in a midcentury villa in a garden shaded by an ancient willow tree (we like to perch on the patio). Launched in 2014 by Spanish-Cuban couple Álvaro Díez, who trained as a sommelier with the Roca brothers (the wine list is impeccable), and Amy Torralbas, whose family owns the property, it serves Caribbean-Med fusion with Asian touches: *salmorejo* with serrano chips; sweet and sour sticky pork ribs with pineapple; and *tocinillo de cielo* with coconut. The furniture was commissioned from local carpenters, walls have been tastefully distressed, the bar is panelled in repurposed wood and the haunting portraits are by Kwang-Sung Park. *Calle 35, 1810 entre 20 y 41, T 203 8315, www.otramaneralahabana.com*

Le Chansonnier

The second incarnation of Héctor Higuera's renowned Le Chansonnier is located in an elegant neoclassical mansion. Times have changed since the original got entangled in red tape – *paladares* can now even buy wholesale. Yet early mornings still see legions of staff on frantic market sweeps, as one will have only oranges and another no onions, or the lorry carrying the eggs hit a pothole. Meanwhile, owners petition Cuba-bound contacts to stuff suitcases with spices. You'd never know it to taste the octopus carpaccio, or duck in olives, from the Frenchified menu here. Interiors match the kitchen's ambition. Bathrooms are camouflaged within Damián Aquiles' scrap-metal installation (above), and the edgy photography and painting is for sale. *Calle J 257 entre 15 y Línea, T 832 1576, www.lechansonnierhabana.com*

On the chalkboard:

EAT MORE
Cream cheese & cascos
de guayabo on toast
(poached guava)   3

LUNCH
Chickpea salad with
homemade flatbread   6
+ slow-roast lamb   9

El Café

Filling a hole in the market, this European-style brunch venue has been a buzzy word-of-mouth smash since 2016. Run by Cuban Nelson Rodríguez Tamayo, who was a chef in London for six years, and wife Marinella Abbondati, it does simple things extremely well, which is no mean feat here. It serves some of Havana's best coffee, fresh juices, honey pancakes, pulled pork in sourdough, vegan dishes, and a signature breakfast plate (when Hurricane Irma wiped out all the island's eggs, El Café invented a sweet-potato hash-brown substitute). Tamayo converted a three-bed apartment in an eclectic 1919 building, making the most of the courtyard patio and high ceilings, and restoring the floral floor tiles; the art is by up-and-coming locals. Open 9am to 6pm.
Amargura 358 entre Villegas y Aguacate,
T 861 3817

El Cocinero

The lease of state property is a lifeline for the city's threatened urban heritage, and a glorious opportunity, as manifested in this savvy industrial conversion above FAC (see p038). The 1913 factory became known as El Cocinero after the peanut-oil company resident here in the 1930s. Up the spiral stairs of its 42m brick chimney, a loungey outdoor area has seating in stone alcoves (with windows through which you can see the action in the club below) and on repro Verner Pantons and BKFs, and a shed-like bar; the more formal interior is hung with art by the likes of Enrique Wong. The menu and sounds are global and voguish, from the Thai chicken satay to a 'drum' of spicy crab and sweet potato, and tunes courtesy of Depeche Mode or Caetano Veloso. *Calle 26 entre 11 y 13, T 832 2355, www.elcocinero.cuba*

7 Días

There are few more chilled perches from which to watch the sun go down than on one of the 'Acapulco' chairs strewn across this granite and marble terrace. It actually used to be a dancefloor, installed with the alfresco bar in the 1950s (and inaugurated with a performance by Nat King Cole) by the owners of this lovely villa designed by Max Borges Recio (see p040), which scooped the national architecture prize in 1941. The laidback restaurant is named after the 2012 movie *7 Días en La Habana* – Kelvis Ochoa and Descemer Bueno composed its soundtrack here and scenes were filmed on the beach in front. An indoor salon is decorated with modern art, but the prime spots are *afuera*, with a platter of seafood from the outdoor grill or fish roasted in the brick oven, and an ice-cold michelada. *Calle 14, 1402 entre 1ra y Mar, T 209 6889*

Efe Bar

Every night, a hipster local crowd saunters up to this cosy townhouse between E and F streets (hence its moniker) on the Vedado main drag. Inside, it's an elongated space with brick walls, a tiled floor, banquettes, graffiti and glitterballs, culminating in a stage with a light installation that changes hues. Here, the roster includes DJs playing global club tracks as well as up-close-and-personal gigs and jams by rising jazz stars.

Scrawled on the mirror behind the bar are cocktail specials that keep the party going until 3am. There's an even more happening scene at Elegua (Aguiar 209; from 10pm) in Habana Vieja, surely the coolest boîte in Cuba, in the former house of a witch doctor, bought by artist Kadir López. It's dark and decadent, with wild informal rumba shows and drag reviews, in a bare concrete shell.
Calle 23, 605 entre E y F, T 835 1857

El Surtidor

The splashiest hotel launch in years, the Kempinski took over an entire block on Parque Central in 2017, with a luxury mall below that seems an affront to Cubans. It is a disconnect from the city, in arguably its best location – but for this reason, the roof bar is hard to top late afternoon for a refined mojito with the unadventurous jetset in their parallel universe.

Gran Manzana Kempinski, T 869 9100

INSIDER'S GUIDE

IDANIA DEL RÍO, DESIGNER

Co-founder of innovative fashion and design label Clandestina (see p094), Idania del Río came here to study when she was 17. 'I loved it,' she says. 'The city has the soul of the sea. Peaceful and fresh on the Malecón at sunset, and chaotic and intense on the streets.' She often starts the day with 'the best coffee in Havana' at El Café (see p055) and, when she has time, checks out the San Isidro (see p088) area – 'an engaging community of creative people' – and the art exhibitions at Galleria Continua (see p068) and Estudio Figueroa-Vives (Calle 21, 303 apto 2 entre H y I, T 832 6332): 'Maybe the best curation of contemporary Cuban work, specialising in photography.'

In the evening, she recommends Café Bahía (Calle 41 entre 14 y 18, T 5294 3285) for seafood and a glass of wine, and then perhaps a cocktail beneath FOCSA in El Emperador (see p010), a 'classic between glory and decay'. Later, she might head to the intimate live bolero venue El Gato Tuerto (see p010) if the 'outstanding' Osdalgia is singing, Pazillo (Calle 5 entre 4 y 6, T 835 1106) for Wednesday's LGBT night, where 'the hosts are hilarious', or Elegua (see p059), 'named after the Yoruba divinity who opens all doors – in this case the doors to dance like there's no tomorrow'. To recover, the roast chicken, rice and beans at El Aljibe (Avenida 7ma y 24, T 204 1584) is 'perfect for curing a hangover', as is a 25-minute trip to the beach at Santa María del Mar: 'This is not Varadero yet it's just perfect.'
For full addresses, see Resources.

ART AND DESIGN

GALLERIES, STUDIOS AND PUBLIC SPACES

Free education, in which the arts, previously a preserve of the elite, were integral, was a vital tenet of Castro's socialist state, and Cuba's cultural output has been extraordinary. The system needed teachers, and established artists assumed a status that endures. In the 1980s, a generation born after the revolution began to use art to challenge the regime, crystallised in seminal 1981 group show 'Volumen Uno' by rising stars including Tomás Sánchez and Flavio Garciandía (see p026). Then, Centro Wifredo Lam (San Ignacio 22 esq Empedrado, T 864 6282) launched in 1983, embracing the country's African roots, and held the first Bienal a year later. Following the collapse of the USSR, private art sales (taxed at 50 per cent) were allowed in 1993. The likes of Los Carpinteros and Kcho were suddenly in the global limelight, and state galleries such as Servando (Calle 23, 1151 esq 10, T 830 6150) and Villa Manuela (see p032) opened in the noughties.

Frustration at official selections for the 2015 Bienal birthed a slew of parallel underground spaces, mostly run on a collective basis out of independent studios and featuring invited collaborators. There's now an alternative arena with a freer ethos, typified by Arsenal (see p022), which displays overseas work, and community-driven Taller Gorría (see p088). Opportunities may be hindered by red tape and a lack of basic materials, an issue stunting a nascent design scene (see p075), but this has driven a unique inventiveness and creativity. *For full addresses, see Resources.*

Galeria Habana

A lone bastion of contemporary art after the revolution, this gallery opened in 1962 and has an impeccale pedigree, launching with a Mariano Rodríguez exhibition, and moving on to Wifredo Lam and the avant-garde – Amelia Peláez (see p067), Fayad Jamis and René Portocarrero. It continues to operate from an incongruous location, an asymmetrical space at the bottom of a residential block on Línea, yet the seven presentations a year are essential viewing. Past shows have included Los Carpinteros' facetious installations, Tonel's text-based work ('Nada que Aprender', above), Carlos Garaicoa's architectural pieces and Yoan Capote's sculptures. It turned commercial in 2001 and today represents mid-career and breakthrough artists such as Roberto Fabelo, Roberto Diago and Esterio Segura.
Línea 460 entre E y F, T 832 7101

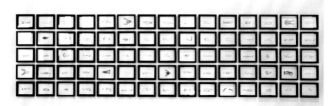

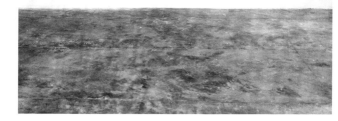

Factoría Habana

This ambitious project, under the wing of the office of the city historian, and curated by Concha Fontenla, has promoted a cross-disciplinary dialogue with Latin America and the world since 2009. The factory is one of cultural creation and collaboration spread over three open expansive floors linked visually by a lightwell and supported by eight imposing pillars. For the Bienal in 2019, 'Intersecciones' brought together 10 contemporary Cuban artists, among them Fernando Rodríguez, Alexandre Arrechea and Rafael Villares, with those from Mexico, Nigeria and South Africa, who used media including sound, video and architectural installation. In 'Old Friends' (above), José A Toirac laid out a broken Woody from *Toy Story* in a glass box as if in a funereal state. *Calle O'Reilly 308 entre Habana y Aguiar, T 864 9518*

Amelia Peláez mural

Welton Becket & Associates' Habana Libre hotel is a modernist landmark that rises up 125m at the highest point of La Rampa. On opening in 1958, it was a strong capitalist statement, so Castro turned the tables 10 months later by choosing its Presidential Suite as his HQ in the early months of the revolution. The 70m-long plinth mural was designed by renowned avant-garde artist Amelia Peláez, in an abstracted geometric style. Titled *Las Frutas Cubanas*, it features a deconstructed hibiscus flower, a symbol of femininity. However, the heavy ceramic pieces were not properly secured and when they began plunging into the pool after just 14 months were removed completely (and subsequently 'lost'). Almost four decades passed before this replica was mounted in 1997, and Havana got its emblem back. *Calle L esq 23*

Galleria Continua
In a 1930s art deco Chinatown cinema and theatre left pretty raw, apart from a subtle Anish Kapoor installation, *When I Am Pregnant*, on the stage wall, Continua launched for the 2015 Bienal. The Italian gallery is the first overseas venture here and works with some 60 artists, including Cubans, nine of whom featured in the engaging 'Cómo Está El Agua?' (pictured). *Rayo 108 esq Zanja, T 5551 6507*

El Apartamento

Outside the official circuit, El Apartamento opened in 2015 as a prototype independent gallery intent on busting genre boundaries, promoting debate and giving 'critical' and exiled artists a presence. It shows a diverse and fascinating mix of work, from pieces created in the 1980s through to those by recent ICA (see p102) alumni, arranged in a series of connected rooms, some with raw concrete floors and ceilings, in an old penthouse in a four-storey midcentury apartment block (buzz to enter). 'El Circuito de Arte Cubano' (above) brought together 15 names including Arlés del Río (*Untitled*, foreground) and Eduardo Ponjuán (*Parasol Azul*, right). On the books are Juan Carlos Alom and Leandro Feal, photographers documenting the reality of today's Cuba. *Apto 3, Calle H 313 esq 15, T 835 6019, www.artapartamento.com*

Galería Acacia

A stalwart of the scene since 1981, Acacia occupies a prime site next to the Capitol in an elongated space stretching through an entire block. It encourages discourse via group exhibitions, and hosts shows by more than 20 artists on its roster, from emerging talent Denis Izquierdo, whose installations often ridicule war, to national prize winners René Francisco, a painter and community activist, and Manuel Mendive, a legend of Afro-Cuban art. His retrospective 'Si Dios y Eleggua Quieren, Todo es Posible' (above) featured nearly half a century of work; for its launch, he body-painted a dance troupe in Parque Central. Prints are sold through the rear entrance on pedestrianised San Rafael. Next door, Collage Habana (T 861 0889) also presents a strong programme. *San José 115 entre Industria y Consulado, T 863 1153, www.acaciagaleria.com*

ARCHITOUR

A GUIDE TO HAVANA'S ICONIC BUILDINGS

The city's architectural history is almost totally intact as urbanism has been stunted for nearly half a century, and economic necessity preserved outstanding stock that anywhere else would have been bulldozed for developers' greed or health-and-safety diktats. Many buildings have fallen down, but those that remain, including the neoclassical villas and flamboyant art deco mansions abandoned by the upper class, have been commandeered and divvied up into multi-family dwellings using screens and improvised mezzanines. Disappointingly, many of the best preserved houses, such as those designed by Mario Romañach and one by Richard Neutra, are now diplomatic residences ensconced on private roads in Cubanacán.

After the revolution, two-thirds of the country's architects left. The idealistic remained and remarkable projects were undertaken, such as the still-popular Habana del Este residential suburb and the ISA (see p076), until the money ran dry and aesthetic austerity won out. Development was then restricted to Soviet-style housing: faceless, prefab blocks in the suburbs and small-scale construction by microbrigades. Today, new builds are limited to hospitals and foreign-sponsored hotels (see p016), although the aim would seem to be financial gain over aesthetic merit. Meanwhile, revolutionary imagery remains an inescapable part of the urban fabric: mantras, slogans and images of Fidel and Che link public and private spaces. *For full addresses, see Resources.*

Edificio Bacardí

The rum company left behind this glorious legacy when it fled Cuba in 1959. The 1930 art deco skyscraper by Esteban Rodríguez Castells, Rafael Fernández Ruenes and José Menéndez is grounded in reddish Bavarian granite and inlaid with brass, adorned with enamelled reliefs in terracotta, including female nudes by Maxfield Parrish, and, of course, crowned by the bat emblem. The exquisite entrance is swathed in veined pastel marble and has a geometric sun-ray floor pattern, etched amber and opaque glass, stucco, cedar and mahogany panels. Head up to the eyrie for 360-degree views before dusk and then imbibe a cubata in the sumptuous maplewood-lined La Barrita (T 862 9310 ext 118; closes 9pm) above the main hall. Detail even extends to the toilet doors' gold leaf and intricate marquetry. *Monserrate 261 esq San Juan de Dios*

Hotel Riviera

After Batista's 1955 tax incentives, mob-run casino hotels shot up in Vedado. Miami architects Polevitzky, Johnson & Associates excelled with these 18 floors of MiMo, built in only six months. It's fronted by Florencio Gelabert's marble sculpture of a mermaid and a swordfish and an elliptical ceramic-clad dome housing the gambling palace, its acoustics designed to augment the sound of clattering chips. The glamour and the Malecón blue faded long ago (although the iconic triple-tiered diving board has been repainted). But public spaces, little altered since Ginger Rogers sang on opening night in 1957, are a mini-museum: the lobby, with its truncated staircase, wooden latticework and wall relief by Rolando López Dirube, is highly evocative. Of the same year and ilk, the Capri (T 833 3747) was reborn in 2014.
Avenida Paseo y Malecón

Lab 26

In a city with so few contemporary builds, this 2015 statement in an unassuming back street is a delightful surprise, and acts as a calling card for the architecture, design and art collective Proyecto Espacios, founded by Vilma Bartolomé in 1998. It's a *casona* reimagined into a stack of white boxes that presents a blank facade, although interiors are accented by darkwood louvered French doors that open onto a garden and a pool,

and a bright-red spiral staircase supported by a circle of poles. A gallery displays PE's furniture, its Havana projects including La Abadia bar – a Malecón intervention (esq Manrique) – and the revamp of hotel San Felipe (see p019), and blueprints, such as a cultural corridor along Línea terminating in the reclamation of a stretch of riverbank.
Calle 26 entre 19 y 21, T 830 6950,
www.proyectoespacios.com

Edificio Arcos

If you happen to be weaving down Calle F at night, be wary of a vertical chasm behind a low wall just off Calle 23. When the Havana expansion proposal was drawn up in 1869, Vedado was virtually uninhabited, dotted with quarries extracting the limestone used to build the city. When it reached here, the grid system was rudely interrupted. In the early 1930s, Edificio Arcos, a concrete and brick tenement block of 71 dwellings, was inserted into one side of the square void. A walkway up a short flight of stairs from the street along its third storey (below the red paint, above) circumvents '*el hueco*' and is used by hundreds of people daily (and has starred in many music videos). The entire structure is in danger of collapse yet state funds go to other often equally demanding but more visible and lucrative projects.
Calle F entre 19 y 21

Cementerio Cristóbal Colón

Havana's cemetery stretches for seven blocks in the centre of town, with its own street grid system and grand architecture, notably the 1936 mausoleum of Catalina Lasa and Juan Pedro Baró (above). French glass master René Lalique, who worked on the couple's Vedado house, Casa de la Amistad (T 830 3114), used Bergamo marble and onyx to fashion a minimalist white cupola, contrasting a black granite door engraved with two praying angels. As the first woman to get divorced in Latin America in 1918 (to be with Baró), Lasa was buried under 6m of concrete so as not to profane the neighbours. Another must-see is the Borges brothers' concrete, tent-shaped, 1957 Núñez-Gálvez tomb. The cemetery is also the resting place of musicians Rubén González and Ibrahim Ferrer and photographer Alberto Korda.

Edificio Solimar

Among the squat architectural hotchpotch and cultural meltdown of Centro rises the eight-storey pink-hued Solimar, dulled and weathered by its namesakes, the sun and the sea. Radical when built in 1944, Manuel Copado's poured-concrete block made fine use of an awkward plot, its stretched form maximising ventilation and light, but ultimately the effects of corrosion too. Overlooking the Malecón, its expressive,

Mendelsohnian walkways evoke the view of the crashing waves. Centro's streets are a riot of art deco and art nouveau facades, although most are in a perilous state. Look up to spot rusting iron grillework, moulded cement bas-reliefs and stylised shopfront logos. You can rent a room in many of these historical gems, including Solimar (hang around below) although it's rather pokey.
Soledad 205 esq San Lázaro

Teatro Bertolt Brecht

Such was architect Aquiles Capablanca's considered approach to the Hebrew Centre, built on a corner site in the mid-1950s, he gave it two completely different faces. On the west facade, offices are protected by brise-soleil, and the synagogue (opposite) is encased in concrete and fronted by an empty volume that supports a hyperbolic arch. This is a private space, yet floating stairs are glimpsed through the glazing.

The north (above) is far more open, and a ramp leads to an auditorium with recessed terraces. This half was bought by the state in 1981 and functions as a theatre. Below it, the low-ceilinged basement Café Brecht is one of the city's most happening scenes and hosts gigs by top contemporary acts like Síntesis and Interactivo on its circular stage. Swing by to see who's playing later.
Calle 13 esq I, T 832 9359

Casa de las Américas

The HQ of the most prestigious of Cuba's many cultural arms is an architectural hybrid – look closely to see the joins. The private house was bought by the American Writers and Artists Association in 1947. An inscrutable volume was plonked on the third floor and Ramón del Busto added the telescopic tower in 1953, creating an ecclesiastical feel, uniting the ensemble with vertical shafts. There are art deco details in the relief map above the canopy entrance, the cupola and four-faced clock. The institution runs a publishing house and promotes Latin American literature and art. Galleries display work from the 1960s to the 1970s, there are rotating exhibitions and past speakers have included Mario Vargas Llosa and Gabriel García Márquez. *Avenida 3ra, 52 esq G, T 838 2706, www.casadelasamericas.org*

Edificio Girón

The location of this 17-storey concrete block comes as a surprise. A slab of Soviet brutalism incongruously overlooking the Caribbean, it has stood defiant since 1967, its presence accentuated by the lack of nearby tall buildings. From afar, this allows an appreciation of Antonio Quintana and Alberto Rodríguez's meticulous design: the parallel lines of the floating stairs, shielded by brise-soleil; the sky bridges; the Googie-style rocket 'feet'; the studs on the supporting walls. As you approach, you notice not only further detail, such as the organic steps of the plinth and the typeface of the Girón sign (the high-rise was named after the bus company that housed its employees here), but also the neglect, perhaps the reason many locals believe it is the ugliest building in Havana. *Malecón entre E y F*

Club Náutico
An overlapping sequence of concrete shells, designed by Max Borges Recio in 1953, allows sunlight into a shaded, airy pavilion. Similar to Borges' earlier Tropicana (see p048), even down to the valets' canopy, Náutico is less wave-like, more giant sea cucumber. After the revolution, it became a club for civil servants. A visit requires a backhander.
Calle 152, Reparto Náutico

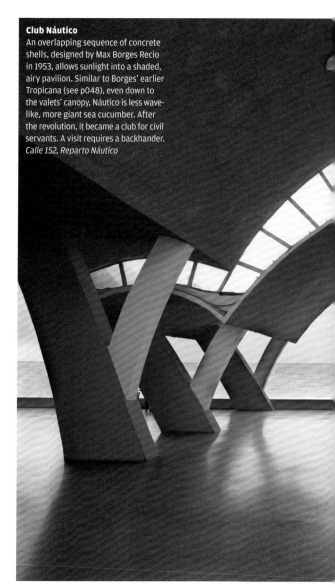

Parada de Puente Almendares

Waiting has long been a way of life here but at least locals have some inspiring spots to do so, a legacy of the Batista government. Havana had an extensive public transport network in the 1950s, and a series of often brightly coloured abstract and sculptural concrete bus stops whose singular designs went way beyond the required function of providing shade from the Caribbean sun. One of the city's finest, making the most of a triangular traffic island (above), is this flamboyant baby-blue construction from 1955 at the intersection of Avenida 47 and Calle 28. Today they're serviced by 'modern' Chinese buses, which replaced the peculiar articulated *camellos* ('camels') towed by truck cabs, a unique Cuban hybrid invented in the fuel shortages of the Special Period to carry as many passengers as possible.
Avenida 47 y Calle 28

Torre Atlantic

If concrete proof were still needed of the inexorable shift in government policy, this 2006 tower on the Malecón was it. Drinkers on the sea wall must have thought they'd had one too many rums as it went up – as nothing had happened here architecturally for decades. Designed by Maurizio Fantoni, it was financed by the Italian developers Bizzi & Partners. The lower volume houses a supermarket and a pharmacy, and the cantilevered tower contains 96 flats, half of which were given to the government in the construction deal. There are two four-bedroom penthouses for rent, pimped-out with every amenity, including jacuzzis and a pool. It's the only option if you're in town to cut an album. Times really have changed these days, as a gargantuan hotel is being built next door and is slated to open in 2021. *Calle D y Ira, www.cubaccommodation.com*

SHOPS

THE BEST RETAIL THERAPY AND WHAT TO BUY

Cuba used to be a retail vacuum, apart from those four must-buys steeped in history: cigars (see p095), rum (see everywhere), art (see p064) and music – seek out the Egrem pressings at Areito (see p048) and vinyl in Seriosha (Neptuno 408). The hub of an emerging arts district, Galería Taller Gorría (San Isidro 214 entre Compostela y Picota, T 864 6713) is run by actor Jorge Perugorría, star of the hit *Fresa y Chocolate*, and hosts performances and gigs, while individual artists' ateliers and showrooms abound, typified by Marcel Molina's epic engravings at Open Studio Molina (Villegas esq O'Reilly, T 862 5164). Film posters (see p092), first-edition books and revolutionary iconography have always made great souvenirs. And if you happen to need something fixing, there is no better place in the world.

Restoration of Habana Vieja has seen the oddly unsettling arrival of Mango and Adidas, and themed stores, only a few of which are worth a look, notably Habana 1791 (Mercaderes 156 esq Obrapía, T 861 3525), which creates bespoke scents, and you can still pick up a classic linen *guayabera* shirt at El Quitrín (Obispo esq San Ignacio, T 862 0810). But the situation is improving due to the new 'private' sector. Contemporary fashion designers are coaxing *cubanas* out of spandex at hip Clandestina (see p094), Dador (Amargura 253) and Capicúa (San Lazaro 55), and Zulu (Aguacate 456, T 763 5831) is providing the accessories with its bags made from leather offcuts. *For full addresses, see Resources.*

Taller Experimental de Gráfica

In most other countries, the equipment in this workshop would either be on the scrap heap or in a museum. In Cuba, things don't work like that – witness the iconic 1950s cars, still running thanks to huge feats of ingenuity, such as using tights for fan belts. The nation has a dynamic graphic-design tradition, and while this warehouse – with its antiquated machinery, wobbly wooden desks and bare bulbs – evokes something from another era (it opened in 1962), the lithographs, woodcuts and zinc and copper engravings that are created and sold here are contemporary and often provocative, and its alumni have pieces in the Museo Nacional (see p026). It offers courses in English for 10CUC an hour (or 200CUC per week). Open 10am to 6pm except Sundays.
Callejón del Chorro, San Ignacio 62, Plaza de la Catedral, T 801 3179

Galería Victor Manuel

Named in homage to Victor Manuel García (see p026), whose 1927 'Exposición de Arte Nuevo' birthed the modern movement in Cuba, this fascinating emporium is a great depository of gifts and mementos. Once a bathhouse, built in 1890, it was restored in 2015, keeping the original marble floor and the bright-blue rafters and shutters that characterise Plaza de la Catedral. Among the numerous paintings, objets d'art and cedar cigar boxes, seek out the landscapes by Ismael Álvarez Abreu, abstract pieces by Bárbaro Reyes Mesa (aka Pango), titanium jewellery by Jorge Gil and sculpture by José Ramón Salas. Also have a browse around the nearby Forma (Obispo 255), run by the Fondo Cubano de Bienes Culturales, which promotes the work of some 35 creatives. *San Ignacio 56, esq Callejón del Chorro, Plaza de la Catedral, T 801 3355*

Assukkar

With a storied history of sugar production, it is no surprise that Cubans have a sweet tooth. Despite the severe dairy shortage due to mismanaged agrarian reforms and failed cross-breeding that decimated the cattle stock (killing a cow has been illegal since 1979), the ice cream at Coppelia (see p031), and *churros*, pastries and desserts, often produced in home kitchens, are wildly popular. Cakes are a status symbol, and at the weekends, elaborate confections are carried through the streets by hand (or on rickshaws bouncing over potholes). There are plenty on offer at this *dulcería*, as well as staples such as *gaceñiga* (sweet bread), *pastelitos de guayaba* (guava) and *ciruela* (plum) and *semifrios* (mousses, flans, etc). It's set in a neo-colonial building with a red-tiled roof opposite Casa de la Música.
Calle 20 entre 33 y 35, T 212 5019

ICAIC
The antithesis of the Hollywood approach, post-revolution movie publicity eschewed individual actors for a conceptual or pop art representation of the *obra* (work) itself. Classic silk-screen posters plaster the walls and ceiling of the ICAIC foyer (pictured); prints, and DVDs of Cuban films, are sold across the road, through the back of the Fresa y Chocolate café bar (T 836 2096). *Calle 23, 1155 entre 10 y 12, T 838 2850*

Clandestina

The forerunner of a nascent Cuban fashion scene, Clandestina was opened by Idania del Río (see p062) and Leire Fernández in 2015 and runs as a collective. It champions sustainability, zero waste, resourcefulness and upcycling, not only out of necessity, but also as an ethos. Its building-site-inspired País En Construcción catwalk show launch featured short-sleeve boiler suits, hazard-tape-style belts and binliner dresses. In the store you will find slogan tees ('Actually, I'm in Havana' was an instant classic), floral button-down shirts, bucket hats, mash-up denim shorts and totes made from salvaged nylon food sacks, as well as graphic posters, design items and an info-map of cool city spots. A hub for the creative community, its facade is painted with a striking mural.
Villegas 403 entre Teniente Rey y Muralla, T 860 0997, www.clandestina.co

Real Fábrica de Tabacos Partagás

Peddling cigars (and everything else) is a full-time occupation for the street-corner characters in Habana Vieja, and while the price will be tempting, the smuggled-out gear may not match its label. The store in the Partagás building, with its flamboyant neoclassical facade, is stocked to the hilt with famous brands including Montecristo and Cohiba and its own range, which has a dense, earthy taste – the unique Culebra (snake) is three cigars intertwined. Veteran staff will advise (you can also try the wares here). Production now takes place at more modern facilities a short walk away at San Carlos 816 (tours from 9am to 1pm except Sundays). Millions of *puros* a year are still made by hand (but not rolled on the thighs of virgins), each employee having a specific task, as a *lector* reads stories and articles.
Industria 520 esq Dragones

ESCAPES

WHERE TO GO IF YOU WANT TO LEAVE TOWN

Many Cubans dream of escape but find it only in music and dance. However, the island itself is enchanting to explore, but don't try to do it in a rush as infrastructure is poor. The Soviet planes have a chilling safety record and although Cuba has the Caribbean's only railway, the train to Santiago, cheekily dubbed the Orient Express, takes 15 hours if you are lucky. At least José Antonio Choy's 1997 Gehry-like station, one of the country's only postmodern builds, provides a startling welcome. The 1950s Chevrolets and Buicks are photogenic but belch and splutter. For longer rides book an official air-con taxi; the two-and-a-half-hour trip to Valle de Viñales, a verdant karst landscape punctuated by steep, flat-topped mogote mountains, caverns and underground lagoons, costs CUC80. The tobacco plantations here supply many of Havana's cigar factories (see p095). Avoid the tourist apartheid at all-inclusive resorts like Varadero, which are about as Cuban as silence. Instead, combine sun worship with history in Trinidad (see p100), from where you can reach the stunning unspoilt coral reefs of Jardines de la Reina.

Alternatively, hire your own wheels and stray off the beaten path. Head to the northern cays, or all the way out west to Maria La Gorda – few road trips are as entertaining, especially if you enter into the socialist spirit and give the locals a lift. There's no traffic but beware of potholes, cows in the fast lane and migrating crabs. *For full addresses, see Resources.*

Club Habana

Most of the original members-only beach and sports clubs on the city outskirts were turned over to the unions, such as nearby Náutico (see p084), but this place remains a domain of diplomats and expats. In its previous incarnation as the Havana Yacht Club, it was so elitist that it turned down President Batista's application because he was mulato. These days, it's open to all, or rather to the few who can bring a foreign passport and afford the CUC25 rate (CUC30 at the weekend), which includes food and drink, and you can often have it almost to yourself. Pass the security and carry on up the drive to Rafael Goyeneche's Beaux Arts 1928 villa. Laze by one of the pools or on the 500m private beach, use the gym, take a sauna or find out if anyone's for tennis. Then pad over to the BBQ for grilled lobster. *Avenida 5ta entre 188 y 192, T 204 5700*

Cienfuegos

Friendships with Cubans in Havana can be infuriating as you can never determine if there's a hidden agenda (assume there is). However, in the provinces, the warmth and curiosity of the locals is unaffected. Leafy, laidback Cienfuegos sits on a peninsula in a natural harbour. Founded in 1819, it was settled by immigrants from Bordeaux and the US French colonies, and its wide boulevards, neoclassical flamboyance and eclectic architecture portray the Gallic approach to urban planning. Built by the cane, the city boomed from 1890 to 1930. Sugar baron Acisclo del Valle brought craftsmen from Morocco to work on his neo-Moorish indulgence, the 1917 Palacio de Valle (T 4355 1003). He died two years later after commissioning another gem: the stately Yacht Club (right; T 4352 6510), of which he was president. Designed by Pablo Donato Carbonell, its inauguration in 1920 attracted the cream of society.

Trinidad

Founded in 1514 on Cuba's south coast, Trinidad was a dozy hamlet until the 18th century, when riches from the sugar trade began to flood in. At one stage, the Valle de los Ingenios was producing a third of the island's crop from 70 mills. Merchants and slave-trade plantation owners turned the city into the colonial jewel it is today, with its grandiose palaces, pastel-painted houses, stained glass and terracotta-tiled roofs, below the 1813 bell tower (above) of the San Francisco de Asís convent. Trinidad is five hours' drive from Havana, so stop off at Cienfuegos (see p098) on the way and, once here, stay awhile. Take a catamaran to paradise island Cayo Blanco de Casilda to snorkel at its pristine coral reef and, by night, dance around the stalactites at Disco Ayala in a beautifully lit cave. Just mind the bats. And we are not talking Bacardi.

Finca La Vigía, San Francisco de Paula
Ernest Hemingway is revered in Cuba. But whether that's because he lived in Havana for 21 years and wrote three books here, most famously *The Old Man And The Sea*, or because he keeps the cash registers ringing, is difficult to fathom. With that in mind, avoid the overhyped Bodeguita and El Floridita, where he used to drink, and head 15km into the suburbs to his house, which remains exactly as it was when he died in 1960. You're not allowed in but peer through the windows at his books, photos, hunting trophies and typewriter, and art by Picasso and Miró. In the grounds is his boat and the pool in which Ava Gardner took a skinny-dip. Have lunch at nearby Las Ruinas (T 643 8286), Joaquín Galván's clever 1972 reappropriation of a sugar mill in Parque Lenin, a relic of Soviet-Cuban ideals.
Calle Vigía y Steinhart, T 691 0809

Escuelas Nacionales de Arte (ENA)

Fidel and Che had a round of golf at the old country club before ripping it up for the National Art Schools. Led by Ricardo Porro, work began with great optimism in 1961, reflected in the expressionism of the five projects: Ballet (pictured) and Music by Vittorio Garatti; Dramatic Arts by Roberto Gottardi, another Italian; and Fine Arts and Modern Dance by Cuban Porro ('I made cupolas in the form of breasts'). A shortage of materials was a blessing: the brick and tile Catalan vaults suited the lush setting. But Soviet diktats on architecture halted work in 1965 with only Porro's schools complete, although four remain in use. This magnum opus is at last being finished in consultation with Garatti thanks to funding from the Getty Foundation. Book a tour in town. *Calle 120, 1110 entre Avenida 9na y 13*

NOTES

SKETCHES AND MEMOS

RESOURCES
CITY GUIDE DIRECTORY

HOTELS

ADDRESSES AND ROOM RATES

Artedel 023
Room rates:
double, from CUC100;
whole penthouse, from CUC380
T 830 8727
www.cubaguesthouse.com

Hotel Capri 074
Room rates:
price on request
Calle 21 esq N y O
T 833 3747
www.nh-hotels.com

Economía 156 022
Room rates:
master room, from CUC150
Economía 156 entre Gloria y Misión
T 861 3211
www.economia156.com

Hotel Florida 019
Room rates:
double, from CUC100
Obispo 252 esq Cuba
T 862 4127
www.gaviotahotels.com

Iberostar Grand Packard 016
Room rates:
double, from CUC120
51 Paseo de Martí
T 823 2100
www.iberostargrandpackard.com

Loma del Ángel 020
Room rates:
Terrace Suite, from CUC320
Cuarteles 104
T 801 5585
www.lomadelangel.com

Malecón 663 027
Room rates:
price on request
Malecón 663 entre Belascoaín y Gervasio
T 860 1459
www.malecon663.com

Meliá Cohíba 016
Room rates:
double, from CUC160
Avenida Paseo entre 1ra y 3ra
T 833 3636
www.meliacuba.com

Palacio del Marqués de San Felipe 019
Room rates:
double, from CUC130
Oficios 152 esq Amargura
T 864 9191
www.gaviotahotels.com

Hotel Parque Central 016
Room rates:
double, from CUC280
Neptuno esq Zulueta
T 860 6627
www.hotelparquecentral-cuba.com

Le Petit Mistinguett 018
Room rates:
price on request
Calle 30, 3112 entre 31a y 33
T 5284 1489
www.lepetitmistinguett.com

Hotel Raquel 019
Room rates:
double, from CUC100
Amargura esq San Ignacio
T 860 8280
www.habaguanexhotels.com

La Reserva Vedado 018
  Room rates:
  double, from CUC180;
  Presidente, from CUC250;
  Coppelia, from CUC280;
  Malecón, from CUC280
  Calle 2, 508 entre 21 y 23
  T 833 5244
  www.lareservavedado.com
Hotel Riviera 074
  Room rates:
  double, from CUC110
  Avenida Paseo y Malecón
  T 836 4051
  www.hotelhavanariviera.com
Hotel Santa Isabel 019
  Room rates:
  double, from CUC150
  Baratillo 9 entre Obispo y Narciso López
  Plaza de Armas
  T 801 1201
  www.habaguanexhotels.com
Hotel Saratoga 017
  Room rates:
  double, from CUC270;
  Habana Suite, from CUC1,150
  Prado 603 esq Dragones
  T 868 1000
  www.hotel-saratoga.com
Torre Atlantic penthouse 087
  Room rates:
  price on request
  Calle D y 1ra
  T 833 0081
  www.cubaccommodation.com

Villa María 023
  Room rates:
  price on request
  T 362 0667
  www.havanacasaparticular.com

WALLPAPER* CITY GUIDES

Author
Jeremy Case

Photography Editor
Rebecca Moldenhauer

Art Editor
Jade R Arroyo

Senior Sub-Editor
Sean McGeady

Editorial Assistant
Josh Lee

Havana Imprint
First published 2007
Fourth edition 2019

ISBN 978 0 7148 7906 2

More City Guides
www.phaidon.com/travel

Follow us
@wallpaperguides

Contact
wcg@phaidon.com

Original Design
Loran Stosskopf

Map Illustrator
Russell Bell

Production Controller
Gif Jittiwutikarn

Assistant Production Controller
Lily Rodgers

Wallpaper* Magazine
161 Marsh Wall
London E14 9AP
contact@wallpaper.com

Wallpaper*® is a registered trademark of TI Media

Phaidon Press Limited
Regent's Wharf
All Saints Street
London N1 9PA

Phaidon Press Inc
65 Bleecker Street
New York, NY 10012

All prices and venue information are correct at time of going to press, but are subject to change.

A CIP Catalogue record for this book is available from the British Library.

PHOTOGRAPHERS

HAVANA
A COLOUR-CODED GUIDE TO THE HOT 'HOODS

PLAZA DE LA REVOLUCIÓN
One million Cubans would often squeeze into this symbolic expanse for a Fidel monologue

MIRAMAR
Boulevards are lined with mansions housing embassies, 'dollar' shops and restaurants

HABANA VIEJA
The colonial core has more than 4,000 listed buildings, ranging from baroque to art deco

LA RAMPA
It's a non-stop hub of classic hotels, cinemas, eateries, fast-food joints and nightclubs

VEDADO
Neoclassical villas and modernist towers are interspersed with cultural centres and parks

CENTRO
The art nouveau gems here have seen far better days but that almost adds to their charm

For a full description of each neighbourhood, see the Introduction.
Featured venues are colour-coded, according to the district in which they are located.